What Is the Story of My Little Pony?

by Kirsten Mayer

illustrated by Andrew Thomson

Penguin Workshop

Dedicated to the three Ms,
who made my time in Equestria magical—KM

For Rhia, Cerys, Esme, and all My Little Pony
fans—AT

PENGUIN WORKSHOP
An imprint of Penguin Random House LLC, New York

First published in the United States of America by Penguin Workshop,
an imprint of Penguin Random House LLC, New York, 2024

Visit us online at penguinrandomhouse.com.

Library of Congress Cataloging-in-Publication Data is available.

Printed in the United States of America

ISBN 9780593226056 (paperback)   10 9 8 7 6 5 4 3 2 1 CJKW
ISBN 9780593226063 (library binding)   10 9 8 7 6 5 4 3 2 1 CJKW

Contents

What Is the Story of My Little Pony?

During 2019, there were over twenty conventions all over the world where fans gathered to celebrate their favorite cartoon show and its stars. Thousands of people celebrated together in cities all over the United States and Europe. Thailand, China, and even Australia hosted events and cruises. One event reached a record of ten thousand attendees! All these people, both grown-ups and kids, were fans of the animated television series *My Little Pony: Friendship is Magic*.

At the events, everyone could attend panels featuring the voice actors from the show and share handmade items such as plush ponies, sparkly nail polish, artwork, and more that were inspired by the animated series.

Many fans made their own costumes to dress up as their favorite character by wearing wigs, unicorn horns, and feathered wings. Some even made hooves to wear over their shoes! A few costumes weren't meant to look like Pony characters, but were inspired by them, using certain colors and symbols such as moons and suns on fancy dresses and capes. Fans were able to show off their creativity and admire everyone else's, too. In fact, one major appeal of these conventions was to simply meet each other, make new friends, and admire the costumes and crafts. Fans wanted to live up to the name of the show and extend friendship to their fellow fans.

For decades, My Little Pony has grown with each generation, reaching around the world and across all ages to build a fan base of millions. From the first little girls who played with them in the 1980s to children today, these classic characters continue to spread a magical message of friendship and empowerment.

CHAPTER 1
A Tale of Three Brothers

My Little Pony figures are produced by a large toy company called Hasbro that also makes games, television shows, and films that are popular all over the world. The huge company it is today has come a long way from its small origins.

The Hassenfeld family immigrated to the United States from Poland. In 1923, brothers Herman, Hillel, and Henry Hassenfeld started a family company in Providence, Rhode Island. At first, they sold leftover fabric pieces, then

started making and selling pencil cases and, eventually, the pencils to go inside them.

HASSENFELD BROTHERS, INC.

Three years later, Hillel left to do other things, and his brother Henry took charge of the Hassenfeld Brothers company with Herman. In the 1940s, Henry introduced some new products—toys! Some of the first toys they sold were doctor and nurse playsets and modeling clay. Soon their toy business was bigger than the pencil business had been. Henry continued to expand not only by creating his own toy ideas, but also by buying ideas from people outside the company.

In 1952, the brothers had their first major hit with a toy called Mr. Potato Head. They had purchased rights to the toy from creator George Lerner. Unlike the modern plastic version, the original set included pieces that kids could push into a real potato. Mr. Potato Head was the first toy to be advertised on television.

The company created some of the toys, bought others from inventors, and grew bigger by buying other companies and their valuable toy and game products. As control passed to a new generation, with Henry's son Merrill taking over, the company eventually became Hasbro, Inc. The Hasbro name is a combination of the two words *Hassenfeld Brothers*.

Hasbro's next big hit was G.I. Joe action figures, first made in 1964. The soldier toys looked like members of the armed forces and were a success as a gift for young boys. Meanwhile, another toy company called Mattel had released one of the most popular toys of all time—the Barbie doll. The team at Hasbro wanted a product to compete with that, a toy that young girls would *love*, something that would feel totally original. Where would that big idea come from?

G.I. Joe

Getting into Action

In the 1960s, the word *doll* was used in the American toy industry to refer to baby dolls or fashion dolls, toys that were intended for girls. Children would pretend to parent the baby dolls and play dress-up with the fashion dolls. With the creation of G.I. Joe, toys that were soldiers, the Hasbro team wanted to both appeal to boys and indicate how they should be played with, and so a company executive created the term *action figure* in 1964. Other toys to be among the first action figures were Marvel and DC superhero figures, and toys made to go with the original Star Wars films. Then He-Man and Transformers toys hit the shelves in the 1980s. Still used today to describe certain toys, *action figure* was first applied to G.I. Joe!

Transformers action figure

CHAPTER 2
A Pony Is Born

How is a toy created? Sometimes one person invents and builds it. More often, a large team of people contributes to the process. Many companies have employees that are part of a research and development team. In a toy company, the team will brainstorm ideas, draw them, build a prototype—or sample—of the toy, and then test it to see if kids like playing with it. Hasbro's team had several ideas they were working on, but one quickly rose to the top of the list.

It was called My Pretty Pony, and the company launched it in 1981. The hard plastic pony was ten inches tall and had mechanisms to swish its tail and wink its eye. The first one was brown. Then pink and yellow versions were released that had designs on the rumps. And then a set with one large

pony and one small baby pony was sold. The pony had a long mane and tail that could be brushed and braided. The idea was that young children could play with this pony much like a fashion doll. My Pretty Pony came with a comb, brush, and other accessories.

Famous Horses

Since the Middle Ages, when the hobbyhorse (a stick with a horse's head at one end) was a popular toy, young people have loved horses and horse stories. Some of the most famous horses came from books.

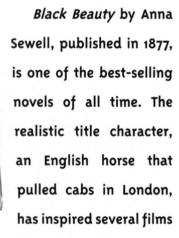

Black Beauty by Anna Sewell, published in 1877, is one of the best-selling novels of all time. The realistic title character, an English horse that pulled cabs in London, has inspired several films and television series from the 1910s to today.

The 1940s brought a trio of successful horse books. The Misty of Chincoteague series of books was based on a real palomino pinto pony. The original books were written by Marguerite Henry, and more titles were published over the course of the next forty-five years. The wild horse in Walter Farley's *Black Stallion* novel also became well-known, inspiring multiple books, films, and television series. *My Friend Flicka,* by Mary O'Hara, in which a boy trains a wild mustang, inspired radio, television programs, and films for over fifty years.

While My Pretty Pony was successful, the team at Hasbro kept working on the idea to make it even better. They made the toy smaller, switched to a softer plastic, and decided to lean into fantasy with a variety of colors that aren't seen on real-life horses. The different colors and the symbols on their rumps would make them collectible, so kids might want to own multiple ponies.

There have always been horse toys and horse stories, but when these colorful ponies came on the scene, they did something different: these weren't realistic horses or realistic stories. These were fantastical creatures living in their own magical world. The choice to move this toy from reality to fantasy was a big deal at the time. Many of the most successful toys had been modeled on children using them to pretend to be adults by role-playing parenting, cooking, working, and dressing up. Kenner's Baby Alive, Mattel's Barbie dolls, and the still-popular Easy Bake Oven were all playthings based on real-life actions that kids saw adults doing. Even G.I. Joe outfits were based on real armed services uniforms and playing with them mimicked an adult military life. Toy trains

Mattel's Barbie doll

and cars were similarly based in reality.

Because of that, the revised pony toys were

a risk. They invited kids to imagine a unique fantasy world while playing with them. Yet the team at Hasbro thought they had the right idea. They released the new line of six smaller, softer, colorful ponies in 1983 under a new name, My Little Pony.

The first six My Little Pony toys were not

Blossom

Cotton Candy

Butterscotch

only new colors—they also had names. They were called Cotton Candy, Blossom, Butterscotch, Minty, Blue Belle, and Snuzzle. As the toy line expanded with playsets, ponies in new poses, and clothes, it grew to eventually include over three hundred different ponies. Toys in this first style, sold until 1992, are referred to as Generation 1.

Blue Belle

Minty

Snuzzle

How Do They Make a Pony?

There are a few different processes for producing plastic toys, but these are the steps for the latest ponies on the shelves.

1. A designer sketches what the toy could look like from multiple angles, including colors and accessories. The rest of the team gives notes, and the sketch is refined.

2. Then a sculptor digitally creates a computer "toy sculpt" to bring the design into three dimensions. (Before computers, this step would be hand sculpted in clay!)

3. The placement of the paint for the pony's features and the color for the hair is finalized. One sample pony gets paint applied and hair attached to the head. A stylist determines the final look for the mane and tail. This sample is kept as the guideline for the ponies that will be produced.

4. An engineering team determines how parts will move and where joints will go, making sure the toy meets safety standards.

5. Packaging and graphics are designed so that the package looks good and the pony can be shipped safely.

6. The ponies are assembled and shipped all over the world to their forever homes!

The 1983 launch of My Little Pony was an instant global hit, and Hasbro rode the success of Generation 1 for almost ten years, expanding the toy line each year. The ponies were sold around the world, and were also manufactured in over a dozen countries with special versions in each place. Ponies could be found in stores from South Africa to Macau, from Peru to Scandinavia, from Australia to India. They even made some Pony Friends. Hasbro released

a giraffe, an elephant, a llama, a lion, a camel, a moose, and even a dinosaur.

Where would Hasbro and the ponies go from here?

Pony Friends dinosaur

CHAPTER 3
A Wild Pony Ride

In the toy world, companies keep things fresh with new products, colors, and stories. Kids always want something new. Trends come and go, styles change, and children grow older.

In the late 1990s, Hasbro tried out a different look for My Little Pony. What came to be called Generation 2 was released in 1997. These Pony toys had longer legs and necks, and they also had a different face design.

These ponies lived in Friendship Gardens—a place that was called Ponyland in Europe—and their world expanded with the first My Little Pony video game. In 1998, the computer game *My Little Pony: Friendship Gardens* hit the shelves. It was on a computer disc with read-only memory (CD-ROM) at a time when games were created on discs that had to be inserted into the computer to be downloaded. In the game, players would feed, groom, and exercise their own pony character. Players could explore a farm and a village with their ponies, and also visit locations like a dance studio and schoolhouse. There were games and puzzles to complete. The pony characters Sundance, Morning Glory, Sweet Berry, Ivy, and Light Heart were featured in the game to interact with the players. This was the first time that the ponies were given more robust personalities for fans to get to know.

The Generation 2 style lasted only a few years, and the creatives at Hasbro were already at work on something new. In the early 2000s another new look was released, later known as Generation 3. (The same characters were also released in a slightly different style, known as Generation 3.5).

This time, there weren't only toys and computer games! The Pony world exploded with characters and stories as it branched out into more toys and

games, animated shows, and even a live musical stage show called *My Little Pony Live!: The World's Biggest Tea Party*.

Each pony's personality became a bigger part of the stories, and girls could pick favorite ponies based on their attitude and not just their appearance.

The first ponies released for Generation 3 were Sparkleworks, Minty, Sweetberry, Wysteria, Kimono, Sunny Daze, Pinkie Pie, and Rainbow Dash. Eventually there were over three hundred ponies to collect in this style!

Rainbow Dash

In 2007, when the Generation 3.5 version of the toys was released, the new look came with a more focused cast of characters featured in all the new stories: Pinkie Pie, Rainbow Dash, StarSong, Sweetie Belle, Scootaloo, Cheerilee, and Toola-Roola.

Scootaloo

My Little Pony grew and grew, and there were many more products created with images of the

 ponies on them. Lunch boxes, bedding, backpacks, party decorations, stickers, watches, and even furniture could be purchased with the colorful Pony world printed all over them. There were more games, music albums, and live shows, and in 2004, the first My Little Pony Fair was held for collectors. My Little Pony became a lifestyle.

New ponies and products were also created around holidays, such as Christmas or Valentine's Day, and one of the favorite new stories was the animated special *A Very Minty Christmas*.

In the show, Minty accidentally breaks the special candy cane that guides Santa to Ponyville, where all the ponies live. It's up to her to save Christmas, but her friends might have to save her on the way to the North Pole!

Pony Personalities

Toola-Roola, Rainbow Dash, Pinkie Pie, Cheerilee,
Scootaloo, StarSong, and Sweetie Belle

There was a huge cast of ponies in both the toys and the animated shows, but these seven were the focus of the Generation 3.5 stories. Several pony character names lived on in later generations, but their personalities were a little different during this time.

• *TOOLA-ROOLA:* She loves decorating and creating

new masterpieces with her skills in arts and crafts.

- *RAINBOW DASH:* She gets up early with excitement for a new day. She loves riding rainbows!
- *PINKIE PIE:* This pony loves surprises and trying new things. She keeps every pony around her laughing and smiling.
- *CHEERILEE:* She loves stories and enjoys reading to her little sister. Her sense of humor keeps her friends laughing.
- *SCOOTALOO:* Always on the go, she loves games and playing outside with her friends—especially her big sister, Cheerilee.
- *STARSONG:* She has a talent for singing and dancing. She loves to be onstage but can be a little shy when she's not performing.
- *SWEETIE BELLE:* The youngest pony, she always sees the bright side of things. She loves sweet treats and sharing them and playing with her friends.

Books were also published during this time with many new stories featuring the ponies. Over one hundred storybooks and activity books brought My Little Pony to girls in a whole new way, further exploring the world. The stories for this new generation took place in Ponyville, filled with unique houses and stores for the ponies. The beautiful Celebration Castle was at the center of town, and its tall towers were featured in *A Very Minty Christmas* as a sign the ponies were home.

Special kinds of ponies were also featured in animated stories: unicorns with horns, Pegasus ponies with wings, and Breezies (tiny ponies with wings and curled antennae).

Perfect Pony Playsets

The pony figures themselves were not the only toys Hasbro produced for My Little Pony. They created dozens of accessory packs and playsets, too. The ponies had hair adornments, hats, boas, outfits, and items like cameras, furniture, and dishes for their homes. The playsets recreated everything from a roller-skating rink to a hair salon to a movie theater. Kids could have their ponies do all sorts of fun things with the additional toys.

The Celebration Castle playset included a toy chest and a hot-air balloon that landed on top of the castle, while the Crystal Rainbow Castle was almost two feet tall and featured a magnet-activated dance floor. There was even a Rainbow Dash pony that came with her own remote-controlled airplane.

Smaller two-inch versions of the ponies were also released with miniature playsets, such as Minty's Christmas Tree, which opened to reveal a cozy little house that had mini hot chocolate mugs!

With all the new toys and stories, it seemed as if the ponies could do anything—just like the girls who played with them. The ponies were keeping up with the idea of "Girl Power," a phrase that was used in the 1990s to indicate that girls could do whatever they liked to do.

As the toys expanded and developed, so did the stories, particularly the TV shows made to introduce girls to the ponies and their world.

CHAPTER 4
Not Just a Toy

It's common now for imaginary film and TV characters to have other products such as toys associated with them. This wasn't always true. In the United States, the Federal Communications Commission (FCC) agency oversaw all the television and cable networks before streaming. Through the decades, television shows made for young people had special rules to follow, and networks were required to air a certain amount of educational and informational shows versus "commercial" content—shows that promoted or advertised something like a toy or food item. Television networks were supposed to file classifications of their programs with the FCC to prove they were following the rules.

When research suggested that younger kids had trouble understanding the difference between advertisements and TV shows, many Americans wanted rules put into place to limit ads and violent content. Over the years these rules were debated and updated, as adults argued over what kids

should be allowed to watch. During the 1980s and 1990s, *My Little Pony* and other shows such as *He-Man and the Masters of the Universe* and *Transformers* were caught up in the controversy. Some people thought these animated shows with related toys were created simply as long commercials for the toys and so they were not appropriate for kids to watch.

In 1984 the FCC dropped many of its guidelines. With fewer rules to worry about, the production of network cartoons exploded.

During the 1980s, there were a lot of animated series created to entertain children. My Little Pony jumped into animated storytelling with a twenty-two-minute special in 1984, then an  animated feature film in 1986, and finally a *My Little Pony* television series (later titled *My Little Pony 'n Friends*) that ran for sixty-five episodes. The initial 1984 special was later cut down and converted into an episode of the series. These were all the same style of animation and included some of the same characters through all the stories.

In the story that launched the TV show, a human girl named Megan travels to the ponies' world to help them defeat different monsters. She has a heart-shaped locket that contains the magic Rainbow of Light, which is a powerful item she uses to defeat an evil centaur and a lava creature later in the series.

Megan

Spike the dragon was introduced in animation for the first time in this series but was different from later versions of the character. The ponies were often seen fighting scary creatures in the 1980s TV show, and the Megan character

Spike

would sometimes ride the pony characters. After this series, the idea of including humans, especially ones who might ride a pony, was dropped. The ponies would handle the magic in future stories.

In 1992, a new television series was created, *My Little Pony Tales*, which ran for twenty-six episodes. This show had a different art style, a song in every episode, and a core cast of seven pony friends: Bon Bon, Bright Eyes, Clover, Melody, Patch, Starlight, and Sweetheart. In this

Starlight

show, there was no human world and no humans. Now the ponies lived in Ponyland with their own society, in which they went to school, babysat their siblings, and hung out at the ice-cream shop. The ponies lived life *like* humans, but no longer *with* humans.

Animation Creation

Animation in the first Pony show was hand-drawn and hand-painted. Two-dimensional (2D) cel animation is an artform that was used to create most animated cartoons and movies before computers were introduced.

Cel is short for celluloid—the sheets that the animation artists would paint and draw on were made of this transparent plastic material.

Cel

Each frame of animation (think one square on a filmstrip) starts with one cel on which the characters are drawn in black ink. Then the reverse side of the cel is painted with the colors behind the black outlines. Backgrounds are hand-painted on separate cels. Then these layers of plastic sheets are stacked together to place the characters over the backgrounds and photographed to create a single frame.

After the 1990s, Hasbro continued to produce film-length animation specials starring the ponies, which briefly played in movie theaters and were then sold on VHS tapes and DVDs for kids to watch at home. *A Very Minty Christmas* was one of these, and other titles included *The Princess Promenade* and *The Runaway Rainbow*, which both feature Ponyville celebrations.

These newer experiments in animation were successful enough to show that the current generation of girls wanted to know more about the ponies. Each film tried something new with the characters and story. And the film plots were different from the stories about the toys themselves. Fans wished they were more similar. It was time for My Little Pony to change again using the lessons learned from the first three generations of toys, books, and television.

In 2009, Hasbro announced they would be working with the Discovery television network to create a new kids' TV channel called The Hub. They were already talking to an exciting animator about a completely new show. My Little Pony was big, but it was about to get even bigger.

CHAPTER 5
That Magic Sparkle

A new generation was about to debut, and this time everything Pony related would initially spring from one creative mind—that of show creator and animator Lauren Faust. She pitched an animated series that would reset and expand

Lauren Faust

the Pony world, with new characters and more complex stories. Faust also developed a new, more modern style for the show's art and design.

Hasbro wanted the storytelling to

be at the center of the My Little Pony world, and they gave Faust the green light to make her vision a reality. The result was the hit animated series *My Little Pony: Friendship is Magic* that debuted in 2010 on The Hub network.

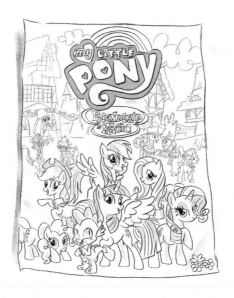

Under Faust's direction, the writers of the show gave the cast of ponies fresh personalities that were complicated, with real strengths and weaknesses, and put them into stories with much more conflict and drama than before.

The show was not only smart and sweet, but also funny, and reflected girls themselves in all their complexity. These were modern ponies for modern girls. And it worked.

My Little Pony: Friendship is Magic was set in a more complex world from the very first episode. The story takes place in the magical land of

Equestria. The ruler of Equestria is the powerful Princess Celestia. Her apprentice, Twilight Sparkle, is sent to Ponyville to learn about friendship. Long ago, Celestia and her sister ruled the kingdom together, but her sister became jealous and turned into the villain, Nightmare Moon.

Princess Celestia

Nightmare Moon

Princess Celestia had to banish her sister, but Twilight Sparkle discovers a prophecy that Nightmare Moon is coming back—and Equestria is in trouble!

Twilight Sparkle soon makes five new friends who help her save the day. As the main six ponies become friends, they learn how to work together to solve any problem and win any battle.

Learning how to be a good friend isn't always easy, and they all learn something through their adventures together. Each of them can wield one of the magical items called the Elements of Harmony—but the magic only works if they are all using them together. Each element is an object that holds some power, but they are the most powerful magical force in Equestria when used together by ponies who embody different aspects of harmony: generosity, honesty, kindness, laughter, loyalty, and magic.

Twilight Sparkle

Lauren Faust (1974–)

Lauren Faust was born in Annapolis, Maryland. After studying animation at the California Institute of the Arts, Faust worked in both film and TV animation as an artist, writer, producer, and director. She worked on the popular series *The Powerpuff Girls* and *Foster's Home for Imaginary Friends* before working on My Little Pony. She then went on to work on the animated series *Super Best Friends Forever* and *DC Super Hero Girls*, among other projects. Faust was thrilled to be approached about My Little Pony because she was a fan herself.

When she was ten years old, Faust had written a letter to Hasbro about wanting to collect all of the Pony toys: "I am WILD over My Little Pony Toys!!!" She wanted to honor that childhood love with the new show, showing there is nothing to

laugh at when it comes to frilly, silly, magical things. Faust wrote, "The child is in there, in each of us. And it's not so hard to find her if we just open our minds to magic."

With Pegasus ponies and unicorns in this world, it's no surprise that other creatures from Greek mythology make appearances on the show, too: hydras, griffins, Cyclopes, Cerberus the

Hydra

three-headed dog, a chimera, and many more.

The "bad guys" in the show were complicated characters, too (and not always that bad). Several even changed their behavior after the ponies

showed them understanding. For example, the ponies together help Nightmare Moon overcome her jealousy and return to Equestria as her true self, Princess Luna.

Princess Luna

Discord is another character who starts as a troublemaker and eventually becomes more friend than foe. The draconequus (a beast with a pony head and mismatched body of other creatures) is a fan of chaos, but he learns he can't fight the Elements of Harmony. Other major villains the ponies fight throughout the course of the show include Queen Chrysalis and her shape-shifting changelings, the magic-stealing centaur Lord Tirek, and the shadowy King Sombra.

Discord

Meet the Mane Six

Lauren Faust established the core group of pony friends in the show, and some of their names were pulled from her childhood memories of earlier

generations—with updated personalities. They are called the Mane Six, a Pony pun on "main." Each of them represents one of the Elements of Harmony; when they work together, they create a power that can defeat the darkest magic.

Fluttershy, Pinkie Pie, Twilight Sparkle, Applejack, Rainbow Dash, and Rarity

- *APPLEJACK:* This farmer is resourceful and dependable, and dearly loves her family. She's honest, practical, and has earned her friends' trust many times over. She represents the element of honesty.

- *FLUTTERSHY:* As her name suggests, she can be shy and nervous, but when it counts, Fluttershy's huge heart leads her to stand up for those who can't defend themselves. She represents the element of kindness.

- *PINKIE PIE:* A free spirit with a sweet tooth. Always giggling, always bouncing, Pinkie Pie is full of energy and ready to celebrate at a moment's notice. She represents the element of laughter.

- *RAINBOW DASH:* With a need for speed, Rainbow Dash can be overly confident, but she's also first in line to help her friends. She represents the element of loyalty.

- *RARITY:* Rarity pays attention to every sparkling detail, especially in her fashion designs. She brings the same attention to her friends. She is a true artist who sees the beauty outside *and* inside. She represents the element of generosity.

- *TWILIGHT SPARKLE:* Twilight Sparkle loves learning, reading, and organizing. Learning about friendship was her biggest challenge yet. She represents the element of magic.

- (*SPIKE:* While not a pony, Twilight Sparkle's peppy assistant dragon is a key part of the group!)

When *My Little Pony: Friendship is Magic* premiered, its core audience of younger girls loved it right away. But then its fan numbers grew as more and more adults tuned in. What initially seemed to many as a silly show just for kids eventually won over older viewers with its clever writing, fun spirit, and memorable songs. The show was critically praised for its stylish storytelling and positive messages. It had top ratings in the United States, Canada, the United Kingdom, and aired across twenty-four networks in 197 territories around the world.

In addition to television episodes of *My Little Pony: Friendship is Magic*, books and comics were published with extra stories about the world and characters, giving fans even more to discover. Some of the books were even written by the writers working on the television show, so everything tied together with the show's details and style. This was also true for the new toys released, which were created in the same design as the animation, with special items matching certain plot details from the show.

In 2010 Hasbro started making mini-figure collectibles that were only a couple inches tall and packaged them with a trading card in a surprise bag—meaning you didn't know which pony was inside until you opened it. Exclusive sets were sold in many stores. Eventually there were

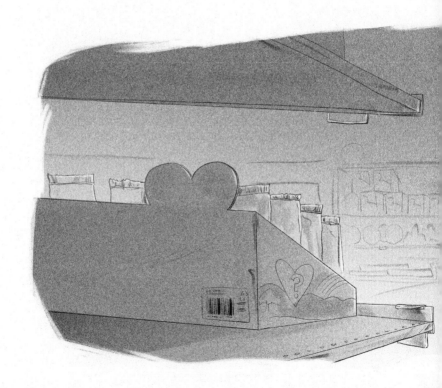

over 1,200 mini figures to collect—that's a lot
of ponies! Many characters from the show were
recreated in tiny form, but many new names and
cutie marks were made to fill out the collections,
too. Some ponies *only* appeared in mini-figure
form.

What's a Cutie Mark?

From the beginning, My Little Ponies have had designs on their rumps, which eventually came to be referred to as cutie marks during Generation 3. The various images made the ponies more collectible and helped distinguish them from one another along with body and mane colors.

It was Lauren Faust who put cutie marks into the stories with *My Little Pony: Friendship is Magic* episodes focused on young ponies anxiously waiting to discover their marks through life experiences. Once a pony figures out what makes them unique—a special talent or a special feeling they radiate—their cutie mark will finally appear.

For example, Pinkie Pie grew up on a very gray rock farm. Her family always looked glum.

After a beautiful rainbow made her smile with joy, she was inspired to throw a colorful surprise party. When her family broke out in smiles, too, her cutie mark of balloons appeared.

CHAPTER 6
My Not-So-Little Pony Fandom

It was a risky move to completely reinvent My Little Pony with a different look, different sensibility, and much more complicated story.

It paid off, though, and soon the television show fandom grew to millions of viewers around the world and included all ages and genders. The very message of the show was embodied by its fan base: all are accepted here.

In 2017, the story of the television series continued in a feature film released in movie theaters, called *My Little Pony: The Movie*. There was a film premiere in New York City, and celebrities walked the red carpet with giant plush ponies.

The film was described as a musical, and the songs were an integral part of both the TV show and the movie. When a character breaks into song on the show, it emphasizes an emotion, raises the stakes in the plot, or highlights a critical turning point. Several songs  are set to well-known tunes or make puns on lyrics that would be recognizable to older fans, such as songs from Broadway musicals, pop songs, or even just the classic tune, "For He's a Jolly Good Fellow."

The *My Little Pony: Friendship is Magic* animated series continued for nine seasons, 235 episodes, and two holiday specials. As characters joined each season, the world expanded and the stories grew more complicated, but the friendship theme was always at its core.

Young girls were the main audience for these Pony stories. Lauren Faust created this show especially for them. She wanted to empower girls to do anything they dreamed of doing. Each generation of girls evolves with the times, and Faust saw new generations as more confident, fair, and eager to be friends with everyone. My Little Pony had grown with its audience.

Yet the animated series expanded beyond its target audience as teens and adults also tuned in to watch the show and decided they loved it. The episodes included jokes and pop culture references to celebrities and shows that older viewers would know, and the songs were well-written catchy tunes. Parents and kids could enjoy the show together.

Some older fans of My Little Pony call themselves Bronies. These fans would go online to discuss the show, and the name *Brony* was created by some of them as a combination of *bro* and *pony*. These viewers really loved the show and its message of friendship appealed to them.

To embrace its larger fan base, Hasbro began using more gender-neutral language for My Little Pony in 2012. This means they didn't limit their marketing to only girls. They knew plenty of boys liked My Little Pony, too!

Bronies and other fans showed their love for all things *My Little Pony: Friendship is Magic* by using their creative abilities to make costumes, create artwork, write stories, write music, and

much more. Fans wanted to get together and celebrate their love for the show, and they started organizing lots of fan conventions all over the world.

Fan conventions have existed for a long time, since the 1930s at least, but have really become popular in the past few decades. A large group of fans get together to meet creators or actors, get autographs, and attend panels to learn more about the thing they love. There are Star Trek and comic book conventions, and in the early 2000s there were My Little Pony conventions.

At first, small groups gathered locally, and then started organizing larger meetups that eventually became full-on conventions. BronyCon brought fans of *My Little Pony: Friendship is Magic* together from 2011 to 2019, PonyCon in the United Kingdom has been gathering all kinds of My Little Pony fans since 2003, and the collector-focused My Little Pony Fair has been running since 2004.

At the conventions there may be special guests, such as voice actors or writers from the show or authors of books. Fans can get autographs from them or ask questions. There are costume contests, games, special screenings of the animation, and more. Collectors may go to find a rare, old pony they don't have or just to see other collections.

Hooves, Horns, and Wings

A guide to all the types of ponies in Equestria.

- *EARTH PONIES:* They have a special connection to animals, plants, and nature, and there is some magic in their ability to work with each. They are physically strong and have good balance.

- *PEGASUS PONIES:* Their wings allow them to fly. Their natural magic also allows them to walk and sit on clouds without falling through, and they can manipulate weather.

- *UNICORNS:* Unicorns have a long pointy horn, which gives them some magic ability, and is useful for popping balloons. Their magic abilities and strengths vary with each individual.

- *ALICORNS:* If a pony has both a horn and wings, they are an alicorn, often a status that is earned with leadership and the title *Princess.* An alicorn has unicorn, Pegasus, and earth pony magic.

- **_SEA PONIES AND MERMARES:_** These underwater pony cousins look like they are part pony and part fish, with lustrous swimming fins that resemble manes and tails. Mermares are somewhat longer than sea ponies, and more reclusive.

Mermares

- **_HIPPOGRIFFS:_** They have beaks and front claws like eagles, and heavily feathered legs. Many hippogriffs were magically transformed into sea ponies to escape a villain who invaded their homeland.

- *BREEZIES:* Breezies look like miniature flying ponies with butterfly wings and antennae. They migrate and carry pollen with them. They love to chatter and fly in swarms, but they can easily be set off course by a gust of wind.
- *BAT PONIES:* Princess Luna's royal guards have bat-like wings and fuzzy ears, and they're generally much darker in color than other ponies.
- *KIRIN:* These ponies have fuller manes, longer ears, and curved horns. Their hooves are cloven. They love to perform, but when they are angry they transform into fiery beasts.

CHAPTER 7
Through the Looking Glass

Even with all the wild success, the team behind My Little Pony was always in motion creating something new. An unusual and big departure from the core line was launched with a whole new toy and animated universe called Equestria Girls. While there weren't any humans in Equestria, these stories featured a parallel dimension where humanlike versions of the Mane Six went to high school. The Equestria Girls are

described as pony girls. They have outfits that are similar to the manes and cutie marks of their pony counterparts.

The story was launched with an animated movie simply called *My Little Pony: Equestria Girls.*

It premiered at the Los Angeles Film Festival in 2013, with a purple carpet event where guests could have pony hair clipped in to their own, get pony face paint, and see a sneak peek at new toys. It was followed by three more films and several shorter animated specials.

Canterlot High

In the first film, when a thief steals Twilight Sparkle's magic crown, she and Spike the dragon follow the trail back through a magic mirror. On the other side is an alternate universe, where instead of ponies there are pony girls. Twilight must fit in at Canterlot High to find her crown.

Equestria Girls continues the tradition of catchy songs and music, even more so than *My Little Pony: Friendship is Magic.*

Several live-action music videos were released featuring the Equestria Girls, and the second film—*Equestria Girls: Rainbow Rocks*—features a battle of the bands. Soundtrack albums were released for the first two films. Books and comics were also published, a mobile game was released, and of course new toys were made. This time Hasbro produced dolls, with new outfits and accessories.

Expanding a Pony world with human characteristics was unusual, but the team wanted to reach older girls, too, and this also allowed them to stretch further with their storytelling. Equestria Girls continued through 2019, alongside *My Little Pony: Friendship is Magic*.

The Voices Behind My Little Pony

One way the different worlds of *Friendship is Magic* and *Equestria Girls* were connected was that they shared the same voice actors for the characters. Voice acting is a special skill that's not quite the same as theater or film acting. Voice actors have only their voices to convey a character, and when voicing animated characters there's often a lot of funny sounds and exaggerated noises they have to make. Singing is often part of the job, too!

A voice actor may record from a script on their own or with other voice actors in the studio with them. They speak or sing into a microphone in a soundproof room. They are asked to do multiple takes, or recordings, for each line to give the filmmakers a variety of performances to choose from for the final piece.

My Little Pony: Friendship is Magic fans love the voice performances of the ponies so much that they give the voice actors behind them celebrity treatment at conventions!

Generation 4.5

As with previous generations, a new smaller look in the My Little Pony toys briefly appeared from 2019 to 2021, referred to as Generation 4.5. The toys were paired with two seasons of animated five-minute shorts called *Pony Life* that featured the same characters from *Friendship is Magic,* but in a different art style and in stories unrelated to the previous show. But after almost ten years, it was time again for a new generation.

CHAPTER 8
A New Generation

In September 2021, a new pony was born when the feature animated film *My Little Pony: A New Generation* premiered on Netflix and ushered in Generation 5. With a new computer-animated art style, Pony toys were once again redesigned with a new head, bigger eyes, and added details. The wings are feathery, the horns have designs on them, and the cutie marks are still there.

For the first time, the stories continue from the previous generation. The ponies and events in Equestria from *My Little Pony: Friendship is Magic* are now in the distant past, considered to be myths. Now the ponies, Pegasus ponies, and unicorns all live apart and are no longer friends. Magic seems to have disappeared. With this jump forward in time, we meet a new group of ponies who go on an adventure to bring back magic and discover friendship along the way. Even one pony can make a big difference.

Generation 5

In 2022, an animated series of shorts debuted online called *My Little Pony: Tell Your Tale*, and a new series (in the style of *A New Generation*) began on Netflix called *My Little Pony: Make Your Mark*. To keep up with today's fans, these ponies are independent and prefer to embrace their uniqueness and stand up for their beliefs. They are open to friendships of all kinds and believe in the fundamental goodness of others.

Meet the Mane Five

There's a new group of ponies featured in *A New Generation*.

- *PRINCESS ZIPP STORM:* This Pegasus loves to perform daring feats and break the rules. She likes to think for herself, and considers honesty the best policy.

- *HITCH TRAILBLAZER:* This pony is the sheriff in Maretime Bay. He takes his duty to protect very seriously, but he can't figure out why other animals love him so much.

- *SUNNY STARSCOUT:* As an earth pony, Sunny wishes she had magic wings to fly or a horn to cast spells. She firmly believes that Pegasus ponies, unicorns, and earth ponies were all once friends—and that they can be again.

- *IZZY MOONBOW:* This unicorn has lots of energy that she uses to invent and craft new things. She

Princess Zipp Storm, Hitch Trailblazer, Sunny Starscout, Izzy Moonbow, and Princess Pipp Petals

loves to make new friends.

• *PRINCESS PIPP PETALS:* Zipp's sister has lots of musical talent and charisma. She's devoted to her fans but is also a loyal sister with a good heart.

In the past, pony characters were crafted in such a way that fans might like one in particular, because they shared a love of one thing. But now, viewers can identify with all the ponies and their complex personalities. There are many different ways to be a person—and many different ways to be a pony.

CHAPTER 9
Memory Lane

The Hasbro company has grown from a small pencil maker into a global entertainment and toy company, and along the way it has learned that stories are very important. My Little Pony stories and characters will continue to evolve and grow, too, because that's what keeps fans happy. And it also creates new fans along the way. Good storytelling inspires fan creativity and art.

The magic of My Little Pony is that anything is possible, as long as friends help each other out.

While the television series *My Little Pony: Friendship is Magic* brought the ponies to new heights, they were successful both before and after. Ponies continue to decorate birthday parties,

adorn backpacks at school, and make excellent costumes. The adorable ponies and their positive messaging are always appealing, no matter what decade it is. Plus, with so many 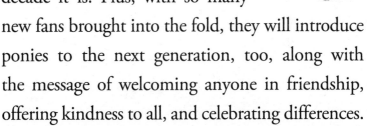 new fans brought into the fold, they will introduce ponies to the next generation, too, along with the message of welcoming anyone in friendship, offering kindness to all, and celebrating differences.

My Little Pony has been around for so long now that different generations of a family remember playing with ponies or watching the shows and love to see their children or grandchildren playing with the modern version. Each family member has their own favorite style of pony.

My Little Pony will continue to inspire girls and fans for years to come. Through entertaining stories, the characters demonstrate positive values of self-acceptance, kindness, and generosity.

Calling All Collectors

Another way all generations of My Little Pony continue to live on is in private collections. Longtime fans love to hunt for older ponies and buy them, and then display them at home. Collecting is one way to show you're a big fan. Rare ponies can be sold for a much higher price than they originally cost! Prices are often determined by how few of the original were made and its condition. Some collectors only want toys that are still in the original packaging, while others don't mind toys that were obviously played with and have some wear on them.

One woman living in the United Kingdom has a collection of over 4,500 ponies! She keeps them displayed in her home in thirteen different bookcases.

The ponies are always more valuable to

collectors if they are still in their original packaging and have all their accessories. These are some of the ponies that collectors would love to find:

• *RAPUNZEL* couldn't be bought in a store—she was only available through the mail, after other Pony receipts were sent in. She has a light pink body and yellow-gold hair with pink streaks. Her mane and tail are very long, and her cutie mark is a girl peeking out of a tower.

- *PRINCESS PRISTINA* is a Pegasus from Generation 1. She has a teal-colored body and neon green hair with tinsel. Her cutie mark is an actual fake gem attached to her instead of just painted on.

- *HIP HOLLY* is from Generation 2 and is called a confetti pony because she has a see-through orange body with confetti-like spots. She has fiery orange hair and came with a purse and a cell phone.

- *THE BIRTHFLOWER PONIES* series from Generation 3 included twelve different ponies, one for each month of the year. They were released in 2006 only at the store Toys"R"Us. Their cutie marks were flowers. From January to December, the ponies were: Carnation, Violet, Daffodil, Daisy, Lily of the Valley, Rose, Larkspur, Gladiolus, Aster, Calendula, Chrysanthemum, Poinsettia.

Everyone is welcome in the My Little Pony world, and everyone can help.

Kids love the characters, parents love the messages, and fans love everything in between.

My Little Pony characters have become instantly recognizable around the world, yet there's still many more magical friendships to come.

Bibliography

*Books for young readers

Connelly, Sherilyn. *Ponyville Confidential: The History and Culture of* My Little Pony, *1981–2016*. Jefferson, NC: McFarland & Company, Inc., Publishers, 2017.

Kaloi, Stephanie. "The Untold Truth Of My Little Pony." The List. Posted October 20, 2021. https://www.thelist.com/637996/the-untold-truth-of-my-little-pony/.

*Skeffington, Miranda. *My Little Pony: Mini Pony Collector's Guide*. New York, NY: Little, Brown Books for Young Readers, 2013.

*Snider, Brandon T. *My Little Pony: The Elements of Harmony: The Official Guidebook*. New York, NY: Little, Brown Books for Young Readers, 2013.

*Snider, Brandon T. *My Little Pony: The Elements of Harmony Volume II*. New York, NY: Little, Brown and Company, 2017.

Websites

mylittlewiki.org

newsroom.hasbro.com

Timeline of My Little Pon

1983	1986	1992	2003	2004	2010	2012

The animated feature film *My Little Pony: The Movie* premieres in theaters June 6

The first My Little Pony Fair, a convention organized by collectors, is held in Las Vegas, Nevada

My Little Pony: Friendship is Magic is nominated for two Daytime Emmy Awards for Outstanding Original Song

My Little Pony is relaunched with new toys and new entertainment set in the town of Ponyville

The first toys are sold under the name My Little Pony

The animated television series *My Little Pony Tales* debuts on the Disney Channel and airs weekly for twenty-six episodes

A brand-new animated series created by Lauren Faust, *My Little Pony: Friendship is Magic*, premieres October 10 in the United States

2013	2016	2017	2019	2020	2021	2022

My Little Pony: Friendship is Magic is nominated for a Daytime Emmy Award for Outstanding Original Song

My Little Pony: Friendship is Magic ends after nine seasons with a ninety-minute finale on October 12

My Little Pony: Make Your Mark series launches

My Little Pony: Equestria Girls premieres on June 16

My Little Pony: A New Generation releases, launching the fifth generation of My Little Pony

The new feature film *My Little Pony: The Movie* makes $61.3 million worldwide

My Little Pony: Pony Life premieres on November 7